Raptor Breeding Season Report for Pinnacles National Monument – 2010

Natural Resource Technical Report NPS/SFAN/NRTR—2011/433

Gavin Emmons

National Park Service
Pinnacles National Monument
5000 Highway 146
Paicines, CA 95043

February 2011

U.S. Department of the Interior
National Park Service
Natural Resource Program Center
Fort Collins, Colorado

The National Park Service, Natural Resource Program Center publishes a range of reports that address natural resource topics of interest and applicability to a broad audience in the National Park Service and others in natural resource management, including scientists, conservation and environmental constituencies, and the public.

The Natural Resource Technical Report Series is used to disseminate results of scientific studies in the physical, biological, and social sciences for both the advancement of science and the achievement of the National Park Service mission. The series provides contributors with a forum for displaying comprehensive data that are often deleted from journals because of page limitations.

All manuscripts in the series receive the appropriate level of peer review to ensure that the information is scientifically credible, technically accurate, appropriately written for the intended audience, and designed and published in a professional manner. This report received informal peer review by subject-matter experts who were not directly involved in the collection, analysis, or reporting of the data. Data in this report were collected and analyzed using methods based on established, peer-reviewed protocols and were analyzed and interpreted within the guidelines of the protocols.

Views, statements, findings, conclusions, recommendations, and data in this report do not necessarily reflect views and policies of the National Park Service, U.S. Department of the Interior. Mention of trade names or commercial products does not constitute endorsement or recommendation for use by the U.S. Government.

This report is also available from the San Francisco Bay Area Network (http://www.nature.nps.gov/im/units/SFAN) and the Natural Resource Publications Management website (http://www.nature.nps.gov/publications/NRPM) on the Internet.

Please cite this publication as:

Emmons, G. 2011. Raptor breeding season report for Pinnacles National Monument - 2010. Natural Resource Technical Report NPS/SFAN/NRTR—2011/433. National Park Service, Fort Collins, Colorado.

NPS 963/106837, February 2011

Contents

Contents (Continued)

Figures

Tables

Appendices

Executive Summary

Pinnacles National Monument ("Pinnacles") provides a diverse habitat for numerous cliff-nesting raptors, including prairie falcons (*Falco mexicanus*), peregrine falcons (*F. peregrinus*) and golden eagles (*Aquila chrysaetos*), as well as a spectacular array of summits and cliff-wall routes for rock-climbers. This monitoring effort was established to determine long-term trends in the number of occupied territories and productivity of nesting prairie falcons. Data on presence and diversity of other nesting raptors are also collected. The effort grew out of a need to reduce potential disturbance that climbers and off-trail hikers may have on cliff-nesting raptors. This report summarizes the results from the 2010 breeding season and represents the 25th year of monitoring at the monument.

To monitor falcons, field technicians survey all potential nest sites three times per breeding season spaced 21-28 days apart. Nests determined to be active were revisited to confirm rearing of nestlings and fledging of young. In 2010, monitoring was conducted from 2 January 2010 until 13 July 2010, with a total of over 150 possible and active nest sites monitored during 884 observation hours.

Prairie falcon occupancy and nesting productivity in 2010 were average compared to the results documented for the previous 25 years of implementing the Pinnacles raptor monitoring program. Thirteen territorial falcon pairs were documented this year with 11 pairs actively nesting. Seven nests successfully hatched and fledged 27 young, and 4 nests failed. Observed nesting productivity during the 2010 breeding season was higher than the 25-year averages for other raptor species nesting in the monument, with 23 breeding pairs representing 9 raptor species in addition to prairie falcons. A peregrine falcon pair successfully nested and fledged 1 young in the Hawkins territory, marking the 6th consecutive year that a successful peregrine falcon nesting effort has been documented at Pinnacles in the last 50 years.

Three golden eagle pairs were observed occupying historical territories at Pinnacles in 2010 but no breeding records were confirmed. Nests for sensitive California species were recorded this season for Cooper's hawks (*Accipiter cooperii*), sharp-shinned hawks (*A. striatus*), and long-eared owls (*Asio otus*). Other nesting raptor species documented in the monument included red-tailed hawks (*Buteo jamaicensis*), red-shouldered hawks (*B. lineatus*), American kestrels (*Falco sparverius*), great-horned owls (*Bubo virginianus*), and barn owls (*Tyto alba*). No raptor detection was confirmed for white-tailed kites (*Elanus leucurus*) in the monument this year.

Acknowledgements

This program would not be as successful as it is without the eyes and ears of helpful Pinnacles employees. Therefore, I would like to thank the NPS employees for their help, encouragement, and passion for the raptors and wildlife diversity at Pinnacles. The many local climbers involved with Friends of Pinnacles also deserve my thanks for their ongoing support of resource protection and breeding raptors at the park and particularly their efforts to publicize and honor advisories in effect. I would also like to extend my appreciation to the monument visitors, for their reports and observations on raptor sightings and for their appreciation and value of the importance of monitoring, managing, and protecting the nesting sites and breeding productivity of raptors in the monument.

I would like to thank Alacia Welch, Daniel George, Dan Ryan, Jess Auer, Scott Scherbinski, Wendy Lanier, Paul Johnson, Brent Johnson, Linda Regan, Jenn Tiehm, Tessa Christensen, and Sarah Reid for contributing valuable observations on raptor territories and pair behavior in the monument. I am also grateful for Denise Louie's and Paul Johnson's support and efforts, in tandem with Marcus Koenen as the manager of the Inventory and Monitoring (I&M) Program, to keep the Pinnacles raptor monitoring program funded annually and on a permanent basis. Marcus Koenen and Paul Johnson provided invaluable support and leadership in producing a finalized peer-reviewed raptor monitoring protocol accepted by the I&M program. Paul Johnson and Sean Mohren also served as editors of the 2010 annual report, contributing greatly to a concise and efficient document consistent with I&M standards.

The following staff shared their experience, excitement, and observations of raptors with me throughout the season, granting me a more complete picture of raptor breeding and diversity at the monument, and assisted in the effective management of raptor advisory areas: Pete Fonken, Debbie Simmons, Michael Rupp, David Soto, Joseph Smith, and Erica Uhor.

Introduction

Pinnacles National Monument ("Pinnacles") is a National Park Service unit located in the Gabilan Mountains of Central California, and provides a diverse habitat for cliff-nesting raptor species, including sensitive species such as prairie falcons, peregrine falcons, and golden eagles. The dramatic landscapes, extensive trails, arrays of summits, and cliff-wall routes at Pinnacles are also used intensively for recreation by rock-climbers and hikers.

Many scientific studies have documented the negative impacts of human disturbance of raptor nest and roost sites, and the resulting nest failures and territorial abandonment associated with these disturbances. Nesting raptor species at Pinnacles sensitive to human disturbance include prairie falcons (Fyfe et al. 1976; Ogden and Hornocker 1977; Harmata et al. 1978; Sitter 1983; Steenhof 1998), peregrine falcons (particularly in remote locations: see Hickey 1942; Bond 1946; Hickey 1969; Steenhof 1998), golden eagles (Newton 1979, 1990; Scott 1985; Steidl et al. 1993; Watson 1997; Steenhof et al. 1997; Kochert et al. 1999), sharp-shinned hawks (Delannoy and Cruz 1988), and long-eared owls (Marks 1986; Marti and Marks 1989; Bloom 1994).

Studies of prairie falcon nest occupancy and productivity have also shown the species to be especially sensitive to human disturbance from mining (Becker and Ball 1981; Bednarz 1984), recreation (Boyce 1982), agriculture (USDI 1979), habitat destruction and nest site limitation (Becker and Ball 1981; Steenhof et al. 1997), and proximity to major roadways (Platt 1974; Boyce 1982).

The main sources of human disturbance of nesting raptors at Pinnacles are visitors that are rock-climbing and hiking on- and off-trail in the monument. Scientific studies have consistently suggested that these recreation activities can be balanced against raptor nesting by establishing closure or advisory areas that act as buffers between human activity and raptor nesting during the breeding season (Fyfe et al. 1976; Olsen and Olsen 1978; Becker and Ball 1980; Suter and Joness 1981; Porter et al. 1987; Holthuijzen 1990; Cade et al. 1996; White et al. 2002). Raptor monitoring program survey data collected at Pinnacles justifies the establishment of climbing/hiking advisories in core areas (high visitor-use areas) each breeding season as a way to protect cliff-nesting raptor species from human disturbance.

The Raptor Monitoring Protocol (Emmons et al. 2010) for Pinnacles National Monument was formally peer-reviewed and approved in 2010. This protocol provides standardized methods and procedures for raptor monitoring at Pinnacles and further details the program specifics. An introduction to the program objectives is briefly described below.

Monitoring efforts began initially to establish annual climbing/hiking advisories in core areas. The program established two long-term monitoring objectives to:

- Track changes in the total numbers of territorial prairie falcon pairs in core areas and non-core areas.
- Track changes in average annual productivity (young of year hatched/pair, young of year at banding age/pair, young of year fledged/pair) in core areas and non-core areas.

Core areas are locations at Pinnacles suitable for prairie falcon cliff-nesting where climbing impacts could occur, based on the presence of historic climbing routes accessible to visitors. Non-core areas refer to all other areas within Pinnacles suitable for cliff-nesting. The core vs. non-core sampling design is detailed further in the Methods section.

A secondary benefit of the monitoring program is that with incidental observations during falcon surveys and a small investment of additional time for area searches during foot travel between falcon activity sites, a substantial amount of information can also be gathered on other raptor species at Pinnacles, particularly sensitive California species that may be impacted by human presence and disturbance in riparian habitats such as: Cooper's hawks, sharp-shinned hawks, white-tailed kites, and long-eared owls. Although lack of consistent nesting data for these species over the course of the 25-year raptor monitoring program precludes statistical and trend analysis, the presence data nevertheless provide valuable information on the diversity and location of breeding raptors at Pinnacles. This has been used for planning purposes relating to the revision of the General Management Plan (GMP), and for guiding timing of routine maintenance activities.

Study Area and Field Methods

Pinnacles is located in the Gabilan Mountains of the central Coast Range of California and encompasses 10,694 hectares (26,425 acres) with elevation ranging from 244 to 1007 meters (800 to 3304 feet). The climate is Mediterranean with hot, dry summers and cool, damp winters. Temperatures range from a mean of 5.2° C in December to 25.2° C in August (41.4° to 77.4° F). The average yearly rainfall is 44 cm (17.4 inches), with the majority of rainfall occurring from November to April (NOAA 2000).

Pinnacles provides a diverse range of habitat types for birds and other species. These habitats include: volcanic rock formations and outcroppings, California mixed chaparral, pine-oak woodlands, grasslands, and riparian habitats.

Sample Design

The prairie falcon monitoring focuses on core areas and non-core areas. Core areas (Figure 1) are locations in Pinnacles that can support prairie falcon cliff-nesting, and where impacts to raptors due to rock climbing activities can occur based on historic rock-climbing use and access. Core area sampling is conducted through a census, because the area is sufficiently small to allow for complete coverage.

Non-core areas refer to all other areas within the monument that can support prairie falcon cliff-nesting. For 2003-2010, non-core area sampling has also been conducted through a census. This has been possible because of comprehensive historical data on prairie falcon nest sites gathered over the past 25 years. In addition, GIS modeling completed in 2008 confirmed that all potential prairie falcon nesting areas in the monument have been surveyed annually during the past 7 years.

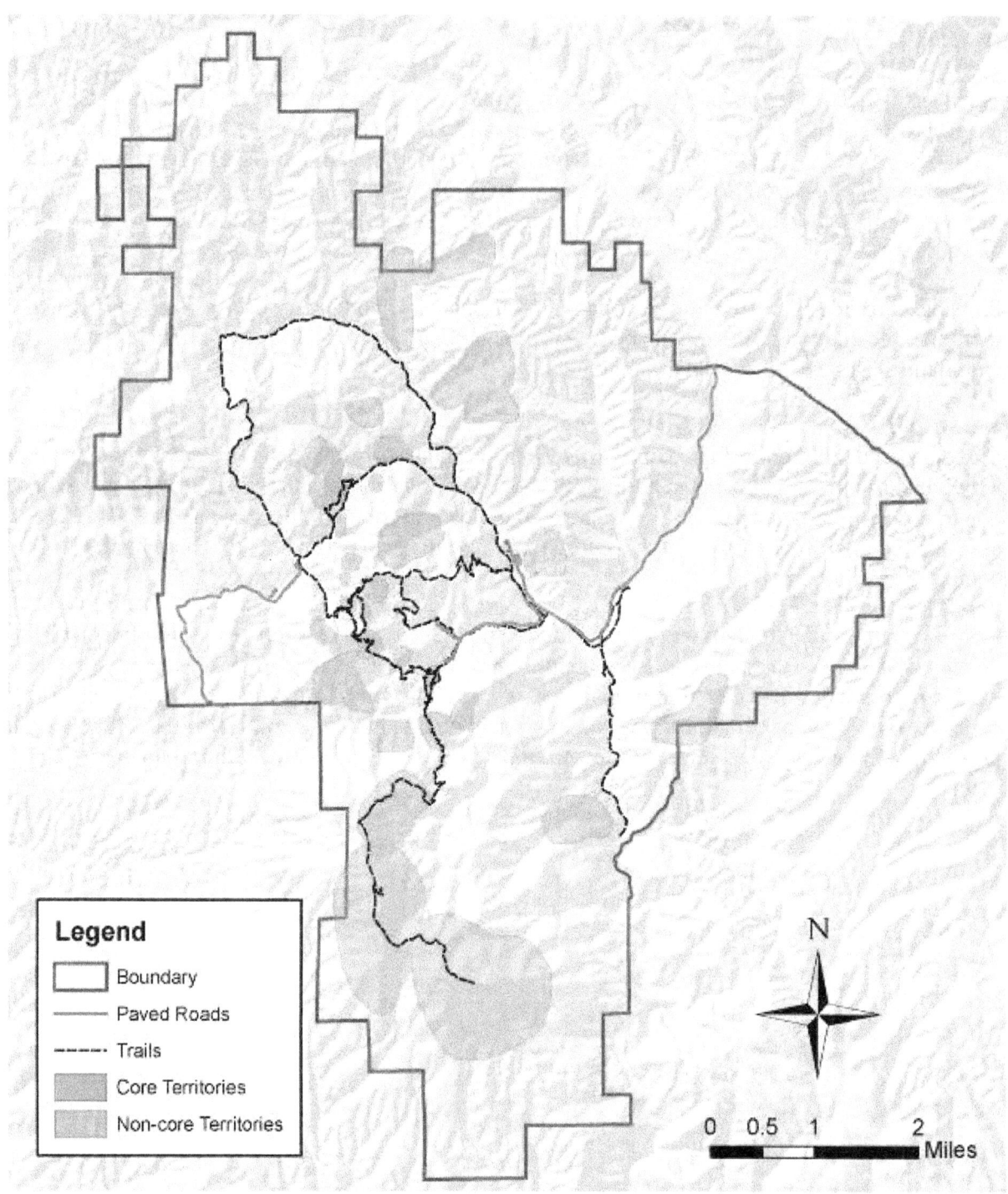

Figure 1. Core and non-core areas at Pinnacles National Monument.

Field Methods

Survey methods followed the standard operating procedures detailed in the Raptor Monitoring Protocol for Pinnacles National Monument, California (Emmons et al. 2010).

Prairie Falcons

Potential and established prairie falcon territories in core and non-core areas were surveyed using Swarovski STS-60 HD 20-60x spotting scopes and Zeiss Victory FL 10x42 binoculars. Observations were made from the locations that provided the best view of an eyrie or a territory. A Magellan Triton 500 GPS unit was used to plot every observation point. Field data were documented with standardized datasheets and field notebooks and the data were entered into a standardized database (Appendix D).

Three- to five-hour observation periods are commonly recommended to document territory occupancy of peregrine falcons and prairie falcons (USFWS 1984; Cade et al. 1996; Smith et al. 2006). Steenhof et al. (1999) employed 2-hour observation periods during point surveys to document territory occupancy of prairie falcons in the Snake River region of Idaho. For a potential prairie falcon territory to be classified as unoccupied at Pinnacles, we adopted a conservative standard of visiting potential nest sites at least three times per breeding season spaced 21-28 days apart to confirm territorial occupancy, courtship, and incubation of eggs within a breeding season (Fuller et al. 1981; Fraser et al. 1983; Steenhof 1998). Survey duration was ultimately dependent upon visibility but at least three 4-hour surveys (12 hours total) were required to verify that "no birds" were present. Nests determined to be active were revisited to confirm rearing of nestlings and fledging of young. Nests in core areas were monitored more frequently and during weekend days when climbers were more likely to be present.

While other monitoring programs infer fledging success at 90% fledge age (Steenhof and Kochert 1982; Anderson and Squires 1997; Steenhof 1998), our protocol was to continue surveys until all young raptors were confirmed as fledged.

During the prairie falcon breeding season status was asserted as follows:

Territories: Territorial behavior included perching, flying, territorial disputes and defense, stooping and scold calling, and roosting locations.

Courtship: Courtship behavior included copulation, food drops and swapping, and potential nest site inspections and preparation.

Incubation: Incubation status was determined by observing prairie falcons flying into a nest hole and not re-emerging for extended periods of time. During this time, egg counts were made whenever possible (e.g. when lighting conditions allowed and when incubating falcons temporarily left the nest during food drops and/or nest switches). Soft incubation – the onset of incubation – was determined by a small number of eggs laid and the female incubating for short durations (15-75 minutes of incubation and 20 minutes or more not incubating the eggs). Hard incubation was characterized by the adult falcons – primarily the females – incubating a full clutch of eggs for hours in duration.

Hatchlings: Hatched young prairie falcons were aged by physical features using an aging guide (Moritsch 1983). Hatch dates were determined by counting backwards from at least two (preferably three or more) independent agings.

Fledging: Fledging was confirmed by seeing young perched and/or in flight away from the nest site. Fledging dates were estimated by the coordination and strength of flight, the size of perches, and the amount of vocalization during flight.

Other Raptors

All data for raptor species other than prairie falcons were collected on ancillary basis. Riparian- and cliff-nesting activity for all species other than prairie falcons was documented en route to observation points for prairie falcon monitoring. Additionally, Pinnacles staff/visitor observations of breeding raptor activity were checked for confirmation of raptor presence.

Potential and established raptor territories were surveyed using spotting scopes (20-60x) and binoculars (10x42). Observations were made from locations where breeding raptor activity was documented and raptor nest sites were most visible. A Magellan Triton 500 GPS unit was used to plot observation points.

For all raptor species other than prairie falcons, potential nesting habitat en route to prairie falcon survey locations were visited at least 2 times per breeding season spaced 21-28 days apart. Visits were scheduled to correspond with general phenology patterns for egg incubation and nesting per species to allow for the highest possibility of confirming territorial occupancy and active nesting of raptor species. Active nest sites were revisited approximately every 28 days to document rearing of nestlings and fledging of young.

Monitoring Schedule

The monitoring season started on 2 January and continued through the end of the nesting season, 13 July (Table 1).

Table 1. Timing of nesting behavior of prairie falcons at Pinnacles National Monument.

Behavior	January	February	March	April	May	June	July
Territorial Falcons							
Courtship Behavior							
Nesting							
Fledging							

Weather was always an important factor. During temperature extremes, heavy fog, or rain, most birds of prey were not active and therefore monitoring was not done during these periods.

Data Management

Data are entered into a MS Access database designed by the Network Data Manager for the San Francisco Bay Area Network Inventory and Monitoring Program. Original data sheets are archived with Pinnacles Resource Management. An annual (static) copy of the Access database is archived on the Golden Gate National Recreation Area computer network drive. Nest data are also submitted to the California Department of Fish and Game (CDFG) California National Diversity Database, and the Santa Cruz Predatory Bird Research Group.

Tabular data in the Results section of this report are derived from queries to the Breeding Raptors and Raptor Observations tables in the MS Access database.

Climbing Advisories

Climbing advisories went into effect by mid-January. Informational signs were established near territories occupied by prairie falcons at least once during the preceding three years. Visitors were advised to avoid these areas but compliance was voluntary. Advisory areas with posted signs (Figure 2) included the Balconies, Hawkins, Scout Peak, Frog/Hand, Discovery Wall, and Little Pinnacles territories.

Figure 2. Setting up advisory sign. ©Gavin Emmons, 2006.

Results

Prairie Falcons

During the 2010 field season, Pinnacles staff spent 500 hours in the field surveying for prairie falcons and volunteers contributed 80 hours of time. The number of prairie falcon nests and productivity this year were consistent with the 25-year running average rates. Eleven prairie falcon pairs attempted to nest this year and seven successful nests produced 27 nestlings and fledglings, compared to 25-year averages of 9.8 nesting pairs, 7.8 successful nests, 28.3 nestlings, and 26.4 fledglings (Table 2).

Occupied Territories

Through the 2010 season 13 territorial pairs of prairie falcons (Figure 3) were confirmed over the course of the breeding season. This number is comparable to the average territorial occupancy of 11.8 territories from 1984-2010 (Table 2). Of these, two pairs did not nest or produce young this year. A single pair actively perched and defended the D. Soto Canyon, High Peaks Trail West of Chalone Housing, and Guard Rock territories through June but did not nest. A second prairie falcon pair occupied the Frog/Hand and Discovery Wall territories but abandoned both by April.

Core Areas: In 2010 there were eight territorial prairie falcon pairs within the core areas. This number is similar to the number of territorial falcon pairs (7.4) in the core areas over the last 25 years.

Non-Core Areas: In 2010 there were five territorial prairie falcon pairs within the non-core areas. This number is similar to the number of territorial falcon pairs (4.4) in the non-core areas over the last 25 years.

Figure 3. Prairie Falcon fledgling at South Balconies. ©Gavin Emmons, 2006.

Table 2. 1984-2010 Pinnacles prairie falcon nesting productivity – core and non-core areas combined.

Year	Territorial Pairs	Nesting Pairs	Successful Nests	# Hatchlings	# Hatchlings / Nest	# Fledglings	# Fledglings / Nest
1984	10	9	8	30	3.8	27	3.4
1987	6	4	4	13	3.3	10	2.5
1988	12	9	8	24	3	24	3
1989	12	12	9	24	2.7	21	2.3
1990	14	10	8	31	3.9	29	3.6
1991	14	11	10	34	3.4	34	3.4
1992	13	11	10	38	3.8	34	3.4
1993	13	12	10	39	3.9	35	3.5
1994	13	13	12	45	3.8	42	3.5
1995	13	11	8	24	3	24	3
1996	12	10	9	35	3.9	34	3.8
1997	12	8	6	26	4.3	26	4.3
1998	10	7	0	0	0	0	0
1999	10	8	6	25	4.2	25	4.2
2000	8	8	7	22	3.1	22	3.1
2001	10	10	7	24	3.4	24	3.4
2002	11	9	7	26	3.7	22	3.1
2003	12	9	8	33	4.1	32	4
2004	12	11	9	36	4	33	3.7
2005	13	10	9	29	3.2	24	2.7
2006	15	14	10	35	3.5	30	3
2007	14	12	9	35	3.9	33	3.7
2008	12	5	4	12	3	12	3
2009	12	11	10	41	4.1	37	3.7
2010	13	11	7	27	3.9	27	3.9
Averages (1984-2010)	11.8	9.8	7.8	28.3	3.5	26.4	3.2

Annual Productivity

Eleven of the 13 prairie falcon pairs nested. Of the 11 nesting pairs, seven had successful nesting events and fledged a total of 27 nestlings (Tables 2, 3). The number of fledglings was typical of the 25-year average of 26.4 fledglings (Figure 4). Four nests failed during the 2010 season, two during egg incubation and two after seven total nestlings hatched.

Table 3. 2010 Pinnacles prairie falcon breeding summary.

Territory	Nest Used/ Last Year Used	# Eggs Laid	# Young Hatched	# Young Known/ Fledged
Drywall	DRY-11/NEW	4	4	4/ 4
Crowley Towers*	CT-1/ 2007	4	4	4/ 4
Pig Canyon	PIG-2/ 2009		0	0
Little Pinnacles*	LP-8/ 2009	3	3	3/ 3
Canyon North of Willow Springs	CNWS-3/ 2005	5	5	5/ 5
South Balconies*	SGB-15/ 2007	4	4	0
Goat Rock*	GOAT-4/ NEW	4	4	4/ 4
Machete Ridge*	MAC-4/ 2009		0	0
Teapot Dome*	TD-3/NEW	3	3	0
South Chalone	SC-7/ NEW	3	3	3/ 3
North Chalone	NC-1/ 2009	4	4	4/ 4

*nests within the core area.

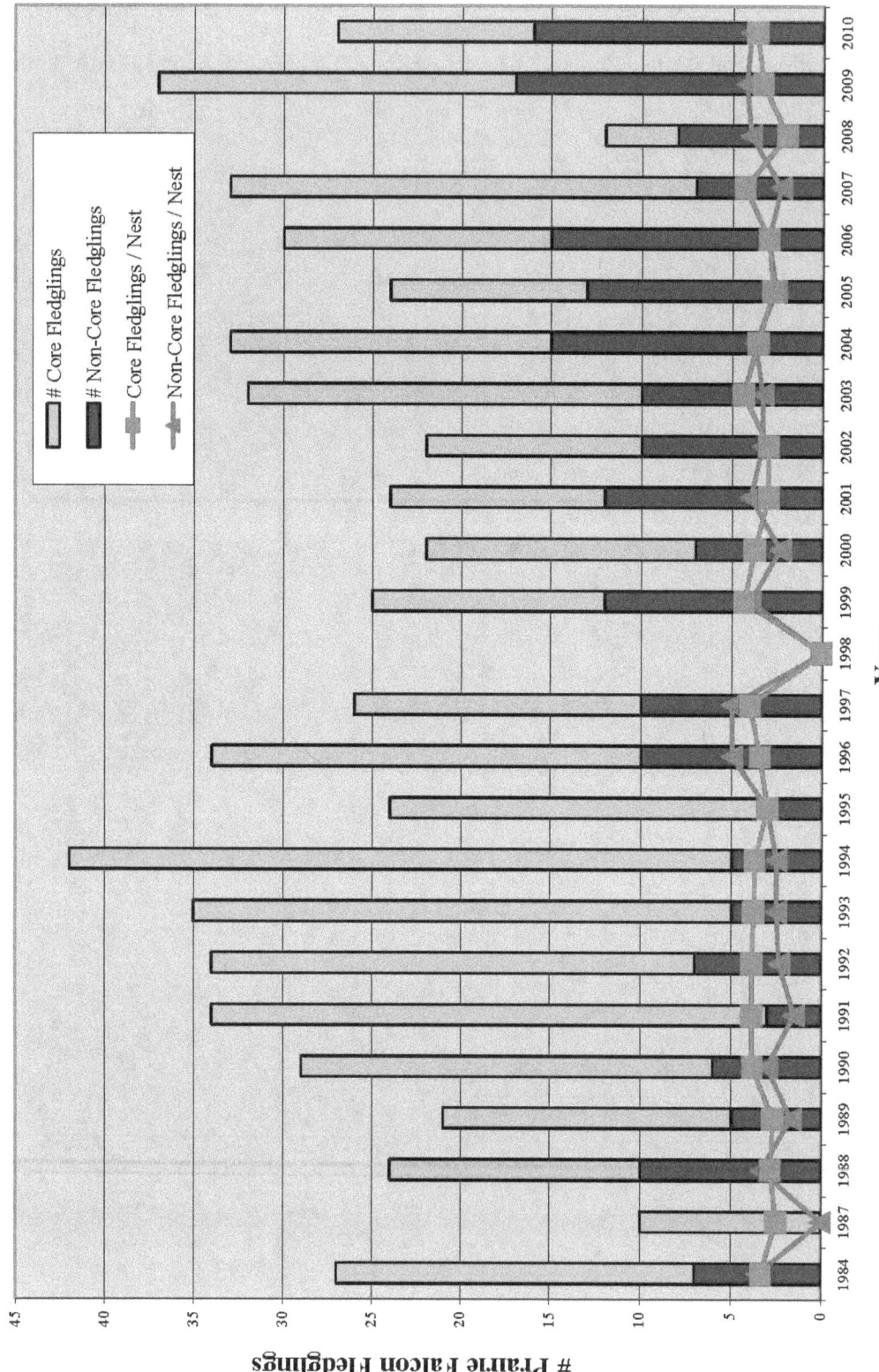

Figure 4. Core vs. Non-Core Pinnacles PRFA Fledgling Productivity, 1984-2010.

Nesting falcon pairs and productivity of nestlings and fledglings per nest within core areas this season were consistent with the 25-year averages. However total successful nests, nestlings, and fledglings were below average due to four documented nest failures. In the core areas only, three successful nest sites produced 11 total fledglings and 3.7 fledglings per nest, compared to the 25-year averages of 5.2 successful nests, 18.0 total fledglings, and 3.3 fledglings per nest (Table 4).

Core Areas: Of the eight territorial falcon pairs in the core areas in 2010, three nested successfully, producing an average of 3.3 fledglings per nest (Table 4). Successful nest numbers are below the 1984-2010 averages of 5.3 successful nests per season and consistent with the averages of 3.3 fledglings per nest.

Non-Core Areas: Of the five territorial falcon pairs in the non-core areas in 2010, four nested successfully, producing an average of 4.0 fledglings per nest (Table 5). These numbers are higher than the 1984-2010 averages of 3.4 successful nests per season and 3.0 fledglings per nest.

Table 4. 1984-2010 Pinnacles prairie falcon nesting productivity – core areas only.

Year	Territorial Pairs	Nesting Pairs	Successful Nests	# Nestlings	# Nestlings / Nest	# Fledglings	# Fledglings / Nest
1984	7	6	6	22	3.7	20	3.3
1987	5	4	4	13	3.3	10	2.5
1988	8	6	5	14	2.8	14	2.8
1989	8	8	6	16	2.7	16	2.7
1990	9	7	6	23	3.8	23	3.8
1991	9	8	8	31	3.9	31	3.9
1992	9	7	7	29	4.1	27	3.9
1993	10	9	8	34	4.3	30	3.8
1994	10	10	10	38	3.8	37	3.7
1995	10	9	7	21	3	21	3
1996	9	8	7	28	4	24	3.4
1997	8	6	4	16	4	16	4
1998	7	5	0	0	0	0	0
1999	6	5	3	13	4.3	13	4.3
2000	5	5	4	15	3.8	15	3.8
2001	7	6	4	12	3	12	3
2002	5	5	4	12	3	12	3
2003	5	5	5	22	4.4	22	4.4
2004	7	7	5	21	4.2	18	3.6
2005	6	5	4	12	3	11	2.8
2006	7	6	5	17	3.4	15	3
2007	6	6	6	26	4.3	26	4.3
2008	7	3	2	4	2	4	2
2009	7	7	6	24	4	20	3.3
2010	8	6	3	11	3.7	11	3.7
Averages (1984-2010)	7.4	6.4	5.2	19.0	3.5	18.0	3.3

Table 5. 1984-2010 Pinnacles prairie falcon nesting productivity – non-core areas only.

Year	Territorial Pairs	Nesting Pairs	Successful Nests	# Nestlings	# Nestlings / Nest	# Fledglings	# Fledglings / Nest
1984	3	3	2	8	4	7	3.5
1987	1	0	0	0	0	0	0
1988	4	3	3	10	3.3	10	3.3
1989	4	4	3	8	2.7	5	1.7
1990	5	3	2	8	4	6	3
1991	5	3	2	3	1.5	3	1.5
1992	4	4	3	9	3	7	2.3
1993	3	3	2	5	2.5	5	2.5
1994	3	3	2	7	3.5	5	2.5
1995	3	2	1	3	3	3	3
1996	3	2	2	7	3.5	10	5
1997	4	2	2	10	5	10	5
1998	3	2	0	0	0	0	0
1999	4	3	3	12	4	12	4
2000	3	3	3	7	2.3	7	2.3
2001	3	4	3	12	4	12	4
2002	6	4	3	14	4.7	10	3.3
2003	7	4	3	11	3.7	10	3.3
2004	5	4	4	15	3.8	15	3.8
2005	7	5	5	17	3.4	13	2.6
2006	8	8	5	18	3.6	15	3
2007	8	6	3	9	3	7	2.3
2008	5	2	2	8	4	8	4
2009	5	4	4	17	4.3	17	4.3
2010	5	5	4	16	4	16	4
Averages (1984-2010)	4.4	3.4	2.6	9.4	3.2	8.5	3.0

Phenology

The first prairie falcon pair was observed at Little Pinnacles on 6 January 2010 (Appendix A). Incubation was first observed at North Chalone Peak on 20 March. The first hatching occurred between 14-16 April at the South Balconies nest. The first fledging took place from 29-30 May at North Chalone. The last fledging took place at Little Pinnacles on 14-16 June when two young fledged from a late season nesting effort.

Other Notes

Seven of the eleven eyries chosen by prairie falcons were used in previous years. All prairie falcon eyries were within historically documented territories. Four nesting attempts failed this year, likely due to predation. Five territories occupied by prairie falcon pairs in the past five years – Pipsqueak Pinnacles, Narrows, Marion Canyon, Tugboat, and Mating Rocks – were vacant this year.

Other Species

During the 2010 field season, Pinnacles staff spent 229 hours in the field surveying for raptors and volunteers contributed 75 hours of time. Observers documented 11 territorial raptor species at Pinnacles in addition to prairie falcons. Of these, nine species were documented as breeding at Pinnacles (Table 6) including four species of concern tracked by the California Natural Diversity

Database (CDFG 2010). The nine breeding raptor species and 23 nest sites documented at Pinnacles in 2010 were generally consistent with averages recorded in the past seven years. For all breeding raptor species other than prairie falcons, eleven previously undocumented nest sites were confirmed.

Throughout the season data were collected on other raptor species nesting at Pinnacles. Notes are presented below. See Appendices B and C for further phenology and breeding data.

Table 6. 2010 Pinnacles nesting productivity for other species than prairie falcons.

Species	Territorial Pairs	Nesting Pairs	Successful Nests	# Fledglings	# Fledglings / Nest
Peregrine Falcon *	1	1	1	1	1.0
Golden Eagle *	2	0	0	N/A	N/A
Red-tailed Hawk	12	7	5	11	2.2
American Kestrel	15	6	2	9	4.5
Red-shouldered Hawk	4	4	3	7	2.3
Cooper's Hawk *	2	2	2	6	3.0
Sharp-shinned Hawk *	2	1	1	3	3
Western Screech-Owl	2	Unknown	Unknown	N/A	N/A
Barn Owl	2	1	1	2	2.0
Great-horned Owl	4	1	1	1	1.0
Long-eared Owl	1	1	Unknown	N/A	N/A

* Species of Concern tracked by California Natural Diversity Database.

Peregrine Falcon

A peregrine falcon (Figure 5) pair occupied and successfully nested in the Hawkins territory, marking the 6th consecutive year that a peregrine pair nested and produced fledglings in the monument. The pair was first observed courting, perching, and circling near Hawkins Peak on 9 January 2010, and chasing a prairie falcon out of the Hawkins territory on 30 January. The pair was previously observed October through December 2009, suggesting the falcons were resident at the monument through the winter season. Through mid-March, the peregrine falcon pair copulated often, inspected historical nest sites at Hawkins regularly, and actively stooped other raptors in the Hawkins territory. The peregrine falcon pair hatched and fledged one young by mid June. Prior to the last 6 years, a previously confirmed peregrine falcon nest effort at Pinnacles was documented in 1957.

Figure 5. Juvenile Peregrine Falcon. ©Gavin Emmons, 2005.

Golden Eagle

Golden eagle pairs were observed occupying historical territories on the west side of North Chalone Peak, at lower Condor Gulch in Pinnacles, and at the Eucalyptus Grove outside of the west entrance of Pinnacles, but no active nest sites were confirmed in 2010. Golden eagle adults and juveniles were active throughout the monument. Historical nest sites in three territories – Frog Canyon, South Chalone Peak, and Eagle Rock – containing five former nest sites were surveyed in mid-winter through late spring, with no new greenery added to any of the nests.

Red-tailed Hawk

Eleven red-tailed hawk (Figure 6) pairs were observed occupying territories at Pinnacles in 2010. Six nesting pairs were confirmed and five pairs successfully produced 11 fledglings. Historical nest sites at the Western Front, South Wilderness (North End)/Grassy Canyon, and Guard Rock were not used this year despite territorial occupation by red-tailed hawk pairs in all of these areas. All six active red-tailed hawk nests were made of sticks and located at Eagle Rock, Hand, Kingman Land North, Lower Condor Gulch, North Balconies, and West Side Entrance. The nest site at Kingman Land North was previously undocumented. The other five nests had been used by red-tailed hawk pairs in previous years. The red-tailed hawk pair at Eagle Rock began egg incubation but failed to hatch any young.

Figure 6. Juvenile Red-tailed Hawk. ©Gavin Emmons, 2005.

American Kestrel

Fifteen territorial pairs and six active nests were confirmed this year. Nesting pairs were observed at Crowley Towers, Discovery Wall, Mating Rocks, Neglected Valley, Pig Canyon, and Resurrection Wall. The Discovery Wall and Neglected Valley nests were documented at historical sites. The other four nests were previously undocumented. The Drywall site hatched young on May 8-10. Nest incubation and hatching dates were not otherwise confirmed. Nine hatchlings were confirmed at two nests: five at Discovery Wall and four at the Mating Rocks nest. At least one fledgling from the Discovery Wall nest and all fledglings from the Mating Rocks nest were confirmed. Other kestrel pairs for which nesting was not confirmed occupied the following territories: Citadel, Drywall, Eucalyptus Grove, Hanging Valley, Kingman Land North, Little Pinnacles, Marion Canyon, South Balconies, and South Chalone Peak.

Red-shouldered Hawk

Four territorial red-shouldered hawk pairs were documented in the monument this year at the following territories: Kingman Land South, McCabe Canyon, Pinnacles Campground, and Bench Area. The Kingman Land South and Pinnacles Campground nests were previously undocumented. Historical territories at Regan Ranch Canyon and South Wilderness Trail were not occupied this year. All nests were built along riparian corridors in pine/oak woodland habitat. The first territorial red-shouldered hawk pair was observed at the Bench Area on 17 February 2010. All four red-shouldered hawk pairs nested this year, with three nests successfully producing fledglings. Seven hatchlings were confirmed at the three successful red-shouldered hawk nests, with full fledge likely at every nest. The Pinnacles Campground red-shouldered hawk pair began egg incubation but failed due to nest abandonment. The Kingman Land South nest produced three hatchlings. Fledging of at least two young was confirmed from the nest and full fledge was likely.

Cooper's Hawk

Two active nests were confirmed for Cooper's hawks (Figure 7) at Pinnacles in 2010. The stick nests were built along riparian corridors in the Marion Canyon and Pinnacles Campground territories. The Marion Canyon nest was last used in 2009, and the Pinnacles Campground nest was previously undocumented. The two Cooper's hawk nests hatched 6 nestlings, with full fledge highly likely from both nests. Historical territories used in 2009 at Kingman Land North, Kingman Land South, and Upper Bear Gulch were not occupied this year.

Figure 7. Cooper's hawk nestling in Marion Canyon nest. ©Gavin Emmons, 2008.

Sharp-shinned Hawk

One sharp-shinned hawk (Figure 8) nest was confirmed at Pinnacles in 2010. The nesting pair was first observed defending the Peaks View Area territory on 5 May 2010 and was confirmed incubating on 27 May 2010. Three nestlings were observed at the previously undocumented nest site, and full fledging was likely by mid-July. The stick nest was located in a pine/live oak grove near the sharp-shinned hawk nests used in the past two years. A sharp-shinned hawk pair was also observed occupying the South Wilderness North territory, but active nesting was not confirmed.

Figure 8. Juvenile sharp-shinned hawk. ©Gavin Emmons, 2003.

Long-eared Owl

One nesting record was documented for long-eared owls (Figure 9) at the park in 2010. A long-eared owl adult was confirmed incubating at a stick nest on a blue oak at the Regan Ranch

Canyon territory on 9 April. Eggs and nestlings were not confirmed, but nestlings were likely and fledglings were possible given observations of substantial feather down at the site and extended adult owl presence at the site in late May.

Figure 9. Long-eared owl adult near Chalone housing area. ©Gavin Emmons, 2006.

Barn Owl

A nesting barn owl pair was documented at a historical site at D. Soto Canyon in 2010. Egg incubation was confirmed on 27 February. Two nestlings hatched on 3-9 April. Fledging of both young was not confirmed but likely by 26 May. Historical sites at Drywall and the High Peaks Trail West of Chalone Housing were unoccupied.

Figure 10. Barn owl nestlings near fledging. ©Gavin Emmons, 2006.

Great-horned Owl

Great horned owls were documented vocalizing and occupying territories at Chalone Picnic Area, High Peaks Trail West of Chalone Housing, Guard Rock, South Wilderness (South End), and Upper Condor Gulch in 2010. The Guard Rock owl pair nested at a previously undocumented cliff-cavity site and hatched one nestling on 14-15 April. The great-horned owl nestling fledged on 7-10 June. Historical territories at Machete Ridge, South Balconies, and Upper Condor Gulch were unoccupied.

Figure 11. Great-horned owl nestling. ©Gavin Emmons, 2009.

Western Screech Owls (Megascops kennicottii)

Screech owls were seen and heard hooting at Upper Bear Gulch and near the Bear Gulch Nature Center beginning in January. No breeding or nest records were confirmed for 2010.

White-tailed Kite

There were no observations of territorial or nesting white-tailed kite pairs documented in Pinnacles in 2010. All six historical territories were unoccupied.

Osprey (Pandion haliaetus)

An osprey was observed soaring over the High Peaks in late March.

Bald Eagle (Haliaeetus leucocephalus)

Bald eagles were occasionally observed near the monument through late spring. An immature eagle was observed feeding sporadically at the Grassy Canyon condor feeding site in January, and an adult was stooped and chased by a prairie falcon adult female at the North Chalone Peak territory.

Discussion

Combined prairie falcon occupancy and productivity in core and non-core areas this year were generally consistent with the 25-year running average rates. Eleven prairie falcon pairs attempted to nest this year and seven successful nests produced 27 nestlings and fledglings, compared to 25-year averages of 9.8 nesting pairs, 7.8 successful nests, 28.3 nestlings, and 26.4 fledglings (Table 2). Based on this relatively consistent occupancy and productivity, the Pinnacles prairie falcon population currently appears to be stable.

In core areas, numbers for successful nests, nestlings, and fledglings were below average in 2010 (Table 4). In non-core areas, respective numbers were above average in 2010 (Table 5). Productivity numbers in the core and non-core areas appeared to be due largely to 4 nest failures, three of which were at core area nest sites. Two core area nest sites failed during development of nestlings, and the remaining nest sites failed during egg incubation. Given the inaccessible locations of the nest sites and lack of any human activity observed at the sites through the breeding season, the nest failures were likely due to predation (e.g. from eagles, ravens, or owls). However, given the lack of constant monitoring at the sites (e.g. through remote video surveillance), nest failure due to human disturbance cannot be entirely ruled out.

For raptors other than prairie falcons, nine breeding raptor species and 23 nest sites were documented at Pinnacles in 2010. Although these numbers are generally consistent with averages recorded in the past seven years, all data gathered for other raptor species were ancillary and are therefore difficult to interpret conclusively.

Conclusion – Management Implications and Recommendations

Climbing management actions, outreach, and recommendations for further management and research are listed below. Refer to Appendix E for further information on public interest highlights for the 2010 season.

Raptors: Climbing Advisories

Climbing advisories were put in place in January in areas with historic climber usage to protect nesting raptors from disturbance. In March and April advisories were updated and lifted in territories that were confirmed unoccupied by prairie and peregrine falcon pairs. Signs detailing climbing advisories were posted at Little Pinnacles, Balconies, Hawkins, Discovery Wall, Scout Peak, Frog/Hand, Crowley Towers, Egg, Tunnel, Teapot Dome, Pipsqueak Pinnacles, and Goat Rock/Resurrection Wall territories.

Due to the large size and climber popularity of Machete Ridge, a partial advisory was instituted at this territory. A partial advisory was also instituted at South Balconies after the nest site was confirmed for the territory, and the General and North Balconies were opened to climber use. Both advisories covered the south half of the cliffs.

All regular advisory signs were affixed to metal brackets and cement foundations to prevent theft, and none were vandalized in 2010. A temporary advisory sign was also placed at the south end of the South Balconies cliffs and was not stolen or vandalized.

In 2010, two incidents of off-trail hikers in advisory areas were documented. No incidents were documented involving climbers.

Condors: Climbing Closures

During the 2010 season a breeding pair of California condors nested at Pinnacles for the first time in over 100 years. Although condors are not a raptor species, their breeding effort did result in climbing management actions at Pinnacles and will be briefly mentioned here. Further details on the Pinnacles condor effort will be covered in a forthcoming condor recovery program report for 2010.

An active condor nest was confirmed at a historical prairie falcon nest site at Resurrection Wall in February 2010 after the adult condor pair was observed incubating an egg. A mandatory climbing closure was put in place in February at Resurrection Wall and Western Front to protect the breeding condor pair from human disturbance. Six temporary closure signs were placed at potential access routes to deter off-trail hikers and climbers near the west end of Goat Rock, the Western Front, and the base of Resurrection Wall. No incidents were observed involving off-trail hikers or climbers.

The nest site failed in March when the condor nestling was evacuated due to observed high blood lead levels and lethargic behavior, and is currently being raised in captivity at the Los Angeles Zoo.

Human / Raptor Interactions And Nest Failures

Prairie and peregrine falcon adults in the Little Pinnacles, North Chalone Peak, Goat/Resurrection, Crowley, Hawkins, Machete, and Balconies territories responded to the presence of on-trail hikers and raptor biologists with agitated behavior by circling and wailing above their respective territories.

Prairie falcon nest entries were conducted at the Little Pinnacles, North Chalone Peak, and Goat/Resurrection nests by the NPS Raptor Biologist, and raptor researcher Douglas Bell from East Bay Regional Park District (see Public Interest Highlights below for further details). All nestlings at these 3 eyries fledged successfully. All falcon nestlings at the Crowley and Hawkins nests also fledged successfully.

Four prairie falcon nest failures were documented at the Machete, Pig Canyon, Balconies, and Egg territories. The Machete and Pig Canyon nests failed during egg incubation, and the Balconies and Egg nests failed when the nestlings at the sites were 2-3 weeks old. Causes of the falcon nest failures in 2010 were not confirmed, but could potentially include nest predation (by ravens, eagles, or owls), abandonment, or significant human disturbance. All 4 nests were not accessible by on-trail hikers. The Pig Canyon, Egg, and Balconies nests had no historic climbing routes directly adjacent to the nest sites. The Machete nest had one rarely used climbing route next to the eyrie but there were no signs of climber use at or near the site throughout the 2010 season.

Education Opportunities

Throughout the year, the raptor biologist and park staff participated in public outreach opportunities to inform visitors about raptor conservation. Educational opportunities included participation in formal events (e.g. Rockpile Rendezvous on May 1-2) and informal events (e.g. visitor contact in high-use areas such as High Peaks, Balconies Cliff Trail, and the Bear Gulch Reservoir).

Management Recommendations

- Continue to establish climbing/hiking advisories in core areas (high visitor-use areas) each breeding season to protect cliff-nesting raptor species from human disturbance.

- Increase information opportunities for visitor use assistants and park rangers to educate park visitors about advisories. Prior to the 2004 season, the park made more attempts to speak with climbers and hikers at trailheads, and to regularly rove on trails to provide interpretation and enforcement of resources.

- Enforce advisories with law enforcement rangers. Although advisories are voluntary, disturbing wildlife is a citable offense that law enforcement rangers should employ to discourage visitors from willfully threatening nesting efforts of breeding raptors at Pinnacles.

- Increase field staff. While the monitoring program focuses on the status and trends of prairie falcons, the park is interested in additional data on non-target species. In order to monitor non-target species adequately, at least 1 other 0.5 FTE field technician is needed during the breeding season.

- Increase use of staff and visitors to observe raptor activity in the field. This can be achieved through regular communication with NPS staff and visitors, bi-weekly monitoring updates on raptor status at the monument, and reminders about filling out wildlife observation cards.

Recommendations for Future Monitoring and Research

Historically, the raptor monitoring program has focused on managing for the protection of cliff-nesting raptors, particularly prairie falcons and golden eagles, because they are species of concern in California and are directly impacted by climbing advisories in the monument. The standardization of raptor monitoring procedures and raptor advisories, and effective communication with hikers and climbers at the monument, has helped to ensure the continuing breeding success of prairie falcons and golden eagles, and the return of breeding peregrine falcons to the monument. However, four sensitive species of concern in California – Cooper's hawks, sharp-shinned hawks, white-tailed kites, and long-eared owls – have received little monitoring attention historically, despite the confirmation of active nesting for all of these species. These four raptor species tend to reproduce along riparian corridors where many of the trails are located and potential disturbance of nest sites by visitors should be studied further. Fletcher (2003) conducted graduate-level fieldwork on accipiter nest site selection and recreational trail use at Pinnacles in 1999-2001. He documented 20 nests and two nest failures along trails in the monument, and recommended further studies to determine the effects of visitor disturbance on accipiter breeding in the monument.

As the staff at Pinnacles continue to transition into managing the bottomlands extending out to Highway 25, the need for further monitoring of forest and woodland nesting raptors becomes even more important. Much of this new monument property contains riparian corridors and oak/pine woodlands suitable for accipiter, kite, and long-eared owl nesting habitat. Recommendations for monitoring of riparian-nesting raptor species include:

- Inventory nest sites for species of concern in riparian habitats in the monument.
- Determine what percentage of riparian raptor nests occur along trails and in high-use visitor areas relative to low-use areas, and how breeding behavior and productivity rates compare in high- and low-use areas.
- Recommend that new trails, buildings, and visitor use areas avoid documented nest sites and likely nesting habitat for riparian raptor species, based on results from inventory and research data above.

Without this baseline information, it may be necessary for resource managers at Pinnacles to enforce seasonal closures of these new developments in order to protect these species from disturbance.

Other recommendations for monitoring and research:

- Conduct an inventory of burrowing owls on recently acquired Pinnacles Ranch property. This owl is also listed as a sensitive species of concern in many western states including California (Martell 1990; James 1992; Haug et al. 1993), with local populations in California – particularly near the San Francisco Bay and the Central Valley – declining steeply in recent years (Johnson 1992). The first record for burrowing owls in the monument was documented in October 2006 on the western boundary near the Bear Gulch Headwaters. These owls may also inhabit the rangeland and fields between the Pinnacles Campground and Highway 25. Field work could be done by a biological science technician or by extending the raptor biologist through September or October.
- Determine potential threats to prairie falcons nesting at Pinnacles. Radio telemetry studies conducted from 2002-2005 revealed important preliminary data about the prairie falcon population at Pinnacles: the population is resident in or near the monument throughout the year, and all radio-tracked falcons fed primarily on prey items just south and west of the monument boundaries, with no evidence of adult falcons feeding north or east of the monument (Buranek 2006). This information suggests that alteration of habitat south and west of the monument boundaries, especially near the town of Soledad, could have significant negative consequences for a viable, long-term population of prairie falcons at Pinnacles. In addition, the effects of pesticide (e.g. rodenticide) in the area are poorly understood.

Literature Cited

Anderson, S. H. and J. R. Squires. 1997. The Prairie Falcon. University of Texas Press. Austin, Texas.

Becker, D. M. and I. J. Ball. 1981. Impacts of surface mining on Prairie Falcons: Recommendations for monitoring and mitigation. Unpubl. rep. Montana Cooperative Wildlife Research Unit, Montana State Univ., Missoula.

Bednarz, J. C. 1984. Effect of mining and blasting on breeding Prairie Falcon (*Falco mexicanus*) occupancy in the Caballo Mountains, New Mexico. Raptor Research 18:16–19.

Bent, A.C. 1937. Life histories of North American birds of prey. Part 1. U.S. National Museum Bulletin 167:95–111.

Bloom, P. H. 1994. The biology and current status of the Long-eared Owl in coastal southern California. Bulletin California Academy of Science 93:1–12.

Bond, R. M. 1946. The Peregrine populations of western North America. Condor 48:101–116.

Boyce, D. A., Jr. 1982. Prairie Falcon fledgling productivity in the Mojave Desert, California. Thesis. Humboldt State University, Arcata, California.

Buranek, S. 2006. Pinnacles Prairie Falcon home range and habitat analysis. Thesis. California State University, Sacramento, California.

Cade, T. J., J. H. Enderson, and J. Linthicum. 1996. Guide to management of Peregrine Falcons at the eyrie. The Peregrine Fund, Boise, Idaho.

California Department of Fish and Game (CDFG). 2010. Special Animals. Online. (http://www.dfg.ca.gov/biogeodata/cnddb/pdfs/SPAnimals.pdf). (accessed 17 Sept. 2010)

Clarke, R. G. 1984. The Sharp-shinned Hawk in interior Alaska. Thesis, University of Alaska, Fairbanks, Alaska.

Delannoy, C. A. and A. Cruz. 1988. Breeding biology of the Puerto Rican Sharp-shinned Hawk (*Accipiter striatus venator*). Auk 105:649–662.

Emmons, G., J. Pettersen, M. Koenen, and D. Press. 2010. Raptor monitoring protocol for Pinnacles National Monument: narrative – version 2.2. Natural Resource Report NPS/ /SFAN /NRR—2010/216. National Park Service, Fort Collins, Colorado.

Fischer, D. L. 1984. Successful breeding of a pair of Sharp-shinned Hawks in immature plumage. Raptor Research 18:155-156.

Fletcher, Clay. 2003. Accipiter nest site selection and recreational trail use effects at Pinnacles National Monument. Thesis. California Polytechnic State University, San Luis Obispo, California.

Fraser, J. D., L. D. Frenzel, J. E. Mathisen, F. Martin, and M. E. Shough. 1983. Scheduling Bald Eagle reproduction surveys. Wildlife Society Bulletin 11: 13-16.

Fuller, M. R. and J. A. Mosher. 1981. Methods of detecting and counting raptors: a review. Studies in Avian Biology 6: 235-246.

Fyfe, R. W. and R. R. Olendorff. 1976. Minimizing the dangers of nesting studies to raptors and other sensitive species. Canadian Wildlife Service Occasional Papers No. 23: 1–17.

Harmata, A. R., J. E. Durr, and H. Geduldig. 1978. Home range, activity patterns and habitat use of Prairie Falcons nesting in the Mojave Desert. Unpubl. rep., Colorado Wildl. Services, Fort Collins, CO for U.S. Department of the Interior, Bureau of Land Management, Riverside, CA. (Contract No. YA-512-CT8-4389)

Haug, E. A., B. A. Millsap, and M. S. Martell. 1993. Burrowing Owl (*Athene cunicularia*). The Birds of North America, No. 61.

Hickey, J. J. 1942. Eastern population of the Duck Hawk. Auk 59: 176–204.

Hickey, J. J. 1969. Peregrine Falcon populations: their biology and decline. University of Wisconsin Press, Madison, Wisconsin.

Holthuijzen, A. M. A., W. G. Eastland, A. R. Ansell, M. N. Kochert, R.D. Williams, and L. S. Young. 1990. Effects of blasting on behavior and productivity of nesting Prairie Falcons. Wildlife Society Bulletin 18:270–281.

Imberski, M. 1998. 1998 Breeding Season Report. Prepared for the National Park Service, Pinnacles National Monument. California. Unpublished.

James, P. C. 1992. Operation Burrowing Owl in Saskatchewan: The first five years. Abstract, Burrowing Owl Symposium. Raptor Research Foundation Annual Meeting, Seattle, Washington, 1992.

Johnson, B. S. 1992. Characterization of population and family genetics of the Burrowing Owl by DNA fingerprinting. Abstract, Burrowing Owl Symposium. Raptor Research Foundation Ann. Meeting, Seattle, Washington, 1992.

Kochert, M. N., K. Steenhof, L. B. Carpenter, and J. M. Marzluff. 1999. Effects of fire on Golden Eagle territory occupancy and reproductive success. Journal of Wildlife Management 63:773–780.

Marks, J. S. 1986. Nest-site characteristics and reproductive success of Long-eared Owls in southwestern Idaho. Wilson Bulletin 98:547–560.

Martell, M. S. 1990. Reintroduction of Burrowing Owls into Minnesota: A feasibility study. Thesis. University of Minnesota, Minneapolis, Minnesota.

Marti, C. D. and J. S. Marks. 1989. Medium-sized owls. Proceedings of the Western Raptor Management Symposium and Workshop. National. Wildlife Federation Science and Technology Series No. 12, Washington, D.C., 1989: 124-133.

Moritsch, M. Q. 1983. Photographic guide for aging nesting Prairie Falcons. United States Department of the Interior, BLM, Snake River Birds of Prey Project. Boise District, Idaho.

National Oceanic and Atmospheric Administration (NOAA). 2000. Pinnacles National Monument station. Climatological Data: California, 1971-2000. National Oceanic and Atmospheric Administration, Washington D.C. Retrieved online from: http://www.ncdc.noaa.gov/normals.html (accessed 17 Sept. 2010)

Newton, I. 1979. Population ecology of raptors. Buteo Books. Shipman, Virginia.

Newton, I. 1990. Birds of prey. Facts on File, Inc. New York, New York.

Ogden, V. T. and M. G. Hornocker. 1977. Nesting density and success of Prairie Falcons in southwestern Idaho. Journal of Wildlife Management 41:1–11.

Olsen, P. and J. Olsen. 1978. Alleviating the impact of human disturbance on the breeding Peregrine Falcon. Ornithologists Corella 2(1): 1–7; and 4(3): 54–57.

Palmer, R. S. 1988. Handbook of North American birds. Vol. 4. Yale Univ. Press, New Haven, Connecticut.

Platt, S. W. 1974. Breeding status and distribution of the Prairie Falcon in northern New Mexico. Thesis. Oklahoma State University, Stillwater, Oklahoma.

Porter, R. D., M. A. Jenkins, and A. L. Ganski. 1987. Working bibliography of the Peregrine Falcon. Nattional Wildlife Federation Science and Technology Series No. 9, Washington, D.C.

Rechtin, J. A.. 1992. Raptor nesting at Pinnacles National Monument: 1984-1992. Pinnacles National Monument. Unpublished. Unpublished report.

Rubine, D. 1995. Climber's guide to Pinnacles National Monument, 2nd Edition. Chockstone Press. Evergreen, Colorado.

Scott, T. A.. 1985. Human impacts on the Golden Eagle population of San Diego County. Thesis. San Diego State University, San Diego, CA.

Sibley, D. A. 2000. National Audubon Society: The Sibley guide to birds. Alfred A. Knopf, Inc. New York, New York.

Sitter, G. 1983. Feeding activity and behavior of Prairie Falcons in the Snake River Birds of Prey Natural Area in southwestern Idaho. Thesis. University of Idaho, Moscow, Idaho

Smith, J. P., and A. Hutchins. 2006. Northeast Nevada Nest Survey 2005. Hawkwatch International, Inc., Salt Lake City, Utah. Retrieved online from: http://www.hawkwatch.org/publications/Technical%20Reports/NNNS%20Report%202005.pdf (accessed 20 Sept. 2008)

Steenhof, K. 1998. Prairie Falcon (*Falco mexicanus*). The Birds of North America, No. 346.

Steenhof, K. and M. N. Kochert. 1982. An evaluation of methods used to estimate raptor nesting success. Journal of Wildlife Management, 46: 885-893.

Steenhof, K., M. N. Kochert, L. B. Carpenter, and R. N. Lehman. 1999. Long-term Prairie Falcon population changes in relation to prey abundance, weather, land uses, and habitat conditions. Condor 101: 28–41.

Steenhof, K., M. N. Kochert, and T. L. McDonald. 1997. Interactive effects of prey and weather on Golden Eagle reproduction. J. Anim. Ecol. 66:350–362.

Steidl, R. J., K. D. Kozie, G. J. Dodge, T. Pehovski, and E. R. Hogan. 1993. Effects of human activity on breeding behavior of Golden Eagles in Wrangell-St. Elias National Park and Preserve; a preliminary assessment, WRST Research and Resource Management Report No. 93-3. National Park Service, Wrangell-St. Elias Natl. Park Preserve, Copper Center, Alaska.

Suter, G. W. and J. L. Joness. 1981. Criteria for Golden Eagle, Ferruginous Hawk, and Prairie Falcon nest site protection. Raptor Research 15: 12–18.

United States Department of the Interior (USDI). 1979. Snake River Birds of Prey special research report to the Secretary of the Interior. Boise District Bureau of Land Management, Boise, Idaho.

United States Fish and Wildlife Service (USFWS). 1984. American Peregrine Falcon Rocky Mountain/Southwest population recovery plan. Rocky Mountain/Southwest Peregrine Falcon Recovery Team, U.S. Fish and Wildlife Service, Denver, Colorado.

Watson, J. 1997. The Golden Eagle. London, United Kingdom.

White, C. M., N. J. Clum, T. J. Cade, and W. G. Hunt. 2002. Peregrine Falcon (*Falco peregrinus*). The Birds of North America Online (A. Poole, Ed.). Ithaca: Cornell Laboratory of Ornithology; Retrieved from The Birds of North American Online database: http://bna.birds.cornell.edu/BNA/account/Peregrine_Falcon (accessed 8 Sept., 2008)

Young, B. 2007. A Climber's Guide to Pinnacles National Monument. Brad Young and Steve Dawson. Twain Harte, California.

Appendix A. 2010 nest phenology and success for prairie falcons.

Nest Species	Territory Occupied	Nest Code	Arrival Date	Begin Incub	Hatch Date	Fledge Date	Abandon Date	Failed Date	# of Eggs	# of Nestlings	Known Fledglings	Possible Fledglings	Occup. Status
PRFA	Ball Pinnacle	*TD	<1/9										Occupied
PRFA	Cyn N of Willow Spgs	CNWS-3	<2/1	<4/8	4/28-5/1	6/2-5			5	5	5	5	Occupied
PRFA	Central High Peaks												Not Occ.
PRFA	Citadel	*MAC	<1/15										Occupied
PRFA	Crowley Drainage												Not Occ.
PRFA	Crowley Towers	CT-1	<1/8	<3/23	4/25-27	5/30-6/1				4	4	4	Occupied
PRFA	D. Soto Canyon	*GR, WCP	<2/11										Not Occ.
PRFA	Deserted Valley	*FROG	<1/24										Occupied
PRFA	Discovery Wall	DRY-11	<1/7	<3/30	4/26-28	6/7-9			4	4	4	4	Occupied
PRFA	Drywall	*TD	<1/9										Occupied
PRFA	Egg												Not Occ.
PRFA	Frog Canyon	*DIS	<1/24										Not Occ.
PRFA	Frog / Hand												Not Occ.
PRFA	Goat Rock	GOAT-4	<1/9	<4/3	4/30-5/2	6/4-6				4	4	4	Occupied
PRFA	Guard Rock	*DS,WCP	<2/11										Occupied
PRFA	Hanging Valley												Not Occ.
PRFA	Hawkins												Not Occ.
PRFA	High Pks W of CPA	*DS,GR	<2/11										Occupied
PRFA	Little Pinnacles	LP-8	<1/6	<4/6	4/26-28	6/14-16			3	3	3	3	Occupied
PRFA	Machete	MAC-4	<1/15	<3/23				<5/7		0	0	0	Failed
PRFA	Marion Canyon												Not Occ.
PRFA	Mating Rocks												Not Occ.
PRFA	Narrows												Not Occ.
PRFA	NE Sec 15	*NC	<1/10										Occupied
PRFA	Neglected Valley												Not Occ.
PRFA	North Balconies												Not Occ.
PRFA	North Chalone	NC-1	<1/10	<3/20	4/17-18	5/29-30				4	4	4	Occupied
PRFA	N. Wilderness Rock												Not Occ.
PRFA	Pig Canyon	PIG-2	<1/14	<4/3				<5/15		0	0	0	Failed
PRFA	Pipsqueak Pinnacles												Not Occ.
PRFA	Prescribed Burn Cliffs												Not Occ.
PRFA	Resurrection Wall	*GOAT	<1/9										Occupied
PRFA	Scout Peak	*GOAT	<1/9										Occupied
PRFA	South Balconies	SGB-15	<1/15	<3/23	4/14-16			5/7-20		4	0	0	Failed
PRFA	South Chalone	SC-7	<3/20	<4/22	4/28-29	6/9-10				3	3	3	Occupied
PRFA	S. Wilderness Rock												Not Occ.
PRFA	Teapot Dome	TD-3	<1/9	<3/26	4/19-21			<5/15		3	0	0	Failed
PRFA	Tugboat												Not Occ.
PRFA	Tunnel	*TD	<1/9										Occupied
PRFA	Upper Bear Gulch												Not Occ.

Nest Species	Territory Occupied	Nest Code	Arrival Date	Begin Incub	Hatch Date	Fledge Date	Abandon Date	Failed Date	# of Eggs	# of Nestlings	Known Fledglings	Possible Fledglings	Occup. Status
PRFA	Upper Condor Gulch												Not Occ.
PRFA	Western Front												Not Occ.
PRFA	Willow Spring Slide	*CNWS	<2/1										Occupied

(Note: for the "Occup. Status" column, # refers to possible fledglings, "Occupied" = territorial occupation, "Not Occ." = no occupation, "Failed" = failed nest, "Abandon" = territory abandoned after confirmed occupancy, "Unknown" = breeding confirmed (see nest code) or likely, but nest status unknown. For the "Nest Code" column, * refers to territorial links for raptor pairs occupying more than 1 territory.)

36

Appendix A. 2010 nest phenology and success for peregrine falcons, American kestrels, golden eagles, and buteos.

Nest Species	Territory Occupied	Nest Code	Arrival Date	Begin Incub	Hatch Date	Fledge Date	Abandon Date	Failed Date	# of Eggs	# of Nestlings	Known Fledglings	Possible Fledglings	Occup. Status
PEFA	Hawkins Peak	HP-5	<1/9	3/18-4/3	4/29-30	6/10-11				1	1	1	Occupied
AMKE	Citadel		<1/15										Occupied
AMKE	Crowley Towers	CT-8		<5/7									Unknown
AMKE	Discovery Wall	DIS-4		<5/22	5/30-31	6/20-21			5	5	1	5	Occupied
AMKE	Drywall		<1/28										Occupied
AMKE	Eucalyptus Grove		<2/7										Occupied
AMKE	Hanging Valley		<5/31										Occupied
AMKE	Kingman Land North		<4/9										Occupied
AMKE	Little Pinnacles		<2/18										Occupied
AMKE	Marion Canyon		<4/10										Occupied
AMKE	Mating Rocks	MAT-2	<3/3	<4/29	5/25-27	6/15-17				4	4	4	Occupied
AMKE	Neglected Valley	NV-2	<3/16		<5/15								Unknown
AMKE	Pig Canyon	PIG-10	<1/14		<5/6								Unknown
AMKE	Resurrection Wall	RW-7											Unknown
AMKE	South Balconies		<3/21										Occupied
AMKE	South Chalone		<3/20										Occupied
GOEA	Eucalyptus Grove		<1/15										Occupied
GOEA	Lower Condor Gulch		<1/16										Occupied
GOEA	North Chalone		<1/2										Occupied
RTHA	Cyn N of Willow Spring		<2/20										Occupied
RTHA	Eagle Rock	ER-2	<3/18	<4/17				<6/17			0	0	Failed
RTHA	Frog / Hand	HAND-1	<1/13	<4/6	4/23-25	6/7-9				1	0	1	Occupied
RTHA	Grassy Canyon		<1/7										Occupied
RTHA	Guard Rock		<3/6										Occupied
RTHA	Kingman Land North	KLN-13	<1/9		4/23-25	6/7-9				2	2	2	Occupied
RTHA	Lower Condor Gulch	*HIPPO	<3/6								2	2	Occupied
RTHA	North Balconies	NB-7	<1/29	<4/17	5/2-5	6/16-17				2	2	2	Occupied
RTHA	South Wilderness Rock		<1/9										Occupied
RTHA	Upper Condor Gulch	HIPPO-2			4/29-5/1	6/16-18				3	2	3	Occupied
RTHA	West Side Entrance	WSE-1		<4/19	4/29-5/1	6/16-18				3	3	3	Occupied
RTHA	Western Front		<2/12										Occupied
RSHA	Bench Area	BA-3	<2/17	<3/19	4/28-30	6/8-10				2	2	2	Occupied
RSHA	Kingman Land South	KLS-8		<3/19	4/8-10	5/25-26				3	2	3	Occupied
RSHA	McCabe Canyon	MC-4		<3/24	4/11-13	5/25-26				2	2	2	Occupied
RSHA	Pinnacles Campground	PCG-3	<2/22	<4/16				<6/9			0	0	Failed
RSHA	Regan Ranch Canyon												Not Occ.
RSHA	South Wilderness Trail												Not Occ.

(Note: for the "Occup. Status" column, # refers to possible fledglings, "Occupied" = territorial occupation, "Not Occ." = no occupation, "Failed" = failed nest, "Unknown" = breeding confirmed (see nest code) or likely, but nest status unknown. For the "Nest Code" column, * refers to territorial links for raptor pairs occupying more than 1 territory.)

Appendix B. 2010 nest phenology and success for accipiters, kites, and owls (barn owls, long-eared owls, great-horned owls, and Western screech-owls).

Nest Species	Territory Occupied	Nest Code	Arrival Date	Begin Incub	Hatch Date	Fledge Date	Abandon Date	Failed Date	# of Eggs	# of Nestlings	Known Fledglings	Possible Fledglings	Occup. Status
COHA	Kingman Land North												Not Occ.
COHA	Kingman Land South												Not Occ.
COHA	Marion Canyon	MAR-4		<4/10	5/16-18	6/14-21				3	2	3	3
COHA	Pinnacles Campground	PCG-4			6/3-6	7/4-8				3	2	3	3
COHA	Upper Bear Gulch												Not Occ.
SSHA	Peaks View Area	PVA-3	<5/5	<5/27	6/16-18	7/9-13				3	2	3	3
SSHA	S Wilderness Trail N		<5/5										Occupied
WTKI	Double Gates												Not Occ.
WTKI	Jawbone Canyon												Not Occ.
WTKI	Kingman Land North												Not Occ.
WTKI	Kingman Land South												Not Occ.
WTKI	Marion Canyon												Not Occ.
WTKI	McCabe Canyon												Not Occ.
WTKI	S Wilderness – N End												Not Occ.
BNOW	D. Soto Canyon	DS-3	<1/31	<2/27	4/3-9	<5/26				2	0		2	2
BNOW	Discovery Wall												Not Occ.
BNOW	South Balconies												Not Occ.
LEOW	Chalone Picnic Area												Not Occ.
LEOW	Kingman Land North												Not Occ.
LEOW	Marion Canyon												Not Occ.
LEOW	Regan Ranch Canyon	RR-3		<4/9									Unknown
GHOW	Chalone Picnic Area	*WCP	<1/13										Occupied
GHOW	Frog Canyon												Not Occ.
GHOW	Guard Rock	GR-3	<1/13		4/14-15	6/7-10				1	1		1	1
GHOW	High Pks W of CPA	*CPA	<1/13										Occupied
GHOW	Machete Ridge												Not Occ.
GHOW	Pig Canyon												Not Occ.
GHOW	Pinnacles Campground		<3/12										Occupied
GHOW	Scout Peak												Not Occ.
GHOW	S. Wilderness – N End												Not Occ.
GHOW	Upper Condor Gulch		<1/14										Occupied
WESO	Upper Bear Gulch		<1/24										Occupied
WESO	Headquarters		<1/9										Occupied

(Note: for the **"Occup. Status"** column, # refers to possible fledglings, "Occupied" = territorial occupation, "Not Occ." = no occupation, "Failed" = failed nest, "Unknown" = breeding confirmed (see nest code) or likely, but nest status unknown. For the **"Nest Code"** column, * refers to territorial links for raptor pairs occupying more than 1 territory.)

Appendix C. Documentation of Changes in Data Collection Methods.

Through the course of the 2010 season, several changes were made to procedures for entering observations into raptor monitoring databases, and relevant sections in the Raptor Monitoring Protocol were revised accordingly. Primarily these changes were put in place to address Inventory & Monitoring standards for data management and storage, and the development of a more efficient workflow and structuring of existing MS Access databases.

Through the 2010 season raptor observations and breeding summaries were entered into the "Breeding Raptors" Access database, after development was finalized in 2007-2008. To increase efficient statistical analysis of prairie falcon occupancy and productivity, additional fields were created in the database "Data Entry" form, including fields detailing detection purpose, survey intention, confirmation of territorial behavior, and prairie falcon detection. Sarah Codde updated and revised legacy data in the Access database to document absence data for prairie and peregrine falcons for the past 25 years of the raptor monitoring program. Dave Press is currently completing Access raptor database revisions to include end-of-season breeding summary queries for number of territories occupied, territorial pairs, nesting pairs, successful nests, total hatchlings, hatchlings per nest, possible fledglings, and fledglings per nest. The revised Access raptor database will be used for data collection and management beginning in the 2011 season.

The 2010 Raptor Monitoring Protocol was peer reviewed by experts in the San Francisco Bay Area Network and accepted as a final document in early 2010, successfully completing a 5-year process of protocol design and revisions.

Appendix E. Public Interest Highlights.

The 2010 breeding season was the 25th year of raptor monitoring at Pinnacles. Field observations began 2 January 2010 and ended 13 July 2010, with a total of over 150 possible and active nest sites monitored during 884 observation hours. Climbing advisories were put into effect in January to reduce nest disturbance by visitors, updated to reflect unoccupied territories in March, and lifted in July at the end of the raptor breeding season.

- The NPS Raptor Biologist conducted prairie falcon nest entries at 3 Pinnacles falcon eyries with raptor researcher Dr. Doug Bell from East Bay Regional Park District, during the 2010 season. All falcon nestlings at the North Chalone Peak, Goat Rock, and Little Pinnacles nests were briefly handled, banded, and blood samples were obtained. All nestlings at these 3 eyries fledged successfully. Banding and blood sample information collected in 2009-2011 will be used to ascertain genetic insularity and pair fidelity in the Pinnacles prairie falcon population.

- Ten breeding raptor species and 34 nests were confirmed in the monument.

- Five sensitive species were confirmed breeding this year: prairie falcon, peregrine falcon, golden eagle, Cooper's hawk, sharp-shinned hawk.

- For the 6th consecutive year a peregrine falcon pair was documented successfully nesting at the monument, producing 1 fledgling. The last previously confirmed peregrine falcon nest effort at Pinnacles was documented in 1957.

- Accipiter species were confirmed nesting in the monument, with the 9th sharp-shinned hawk nest ever documented.

- Eighteen breeding records for raptor species at Pinnacles were reported to the Santa Cruz Predatory Bird Research Group and the California Natural Diversity Database (through the California Department of Fish and Game).

- An ArcMap project was updated to visually display GPS and GIS information relating to the raptor monitoring program, including historical nest sites, monitoring watch spots, nest distribution by geologic and habitat layers, and locations of advisory signs posted at Pinnacles.

- All raptor advisory signs were affixed to metal brackets in cement foundations to make the signs more secure and to prevent their theft and movement.

- The third annual Rockpile Rendezvous – a centennial event to emphasize climber contributions, history, and management at Pinnacles over the past 60 years – was organized by the raptor biologist and other monument staff, drawing in the local climbing community and providing visitors with information on historical resource and recreation management at the monument.

- The Raptor Monitoring Protocol was submitted to and accepted by peer reviewers with the SFAN Inventory and Monitoring network, concluding 5 years of protocol and manuscript development.

NPS 963/106837, February 2011